Be wealthy

Unlocking the Secrets to Financial Freedom and Abundance

Sharatth Sunkaran

To my beloved family,

You have been my constant source of love, support, and encouragement throughout my life. Your unwavering belief in me and my dreams has pushed me to pursue my passions and strive for excellence.

This book is a tribute to you, for everything you have done for me. Your sacrifices, guidance, and unconditional love have shaped me into the person I am today. I am forever grateful for your presence in my life.

Thank you for being my rock and for always standing by me. This book is dedicated to you with all my heart.

Love always,
Sharatth Sunkaran

Contents

Title Page
Dedication
Preface
Chapter 1: 4
Chapter 2: 10
Chapter 3: 15
Chapter 4: 20
Chapter 5: 26
Chapter 6: 32
Chapter 7: 38
Chapter 8: 44

Preface

The purpose of the book "Be Wealthy" is to provide readers with the knowledge, skills, and mindset necessary to achieve financial success and live a life of abundance. The book is not just about accumulating wealth, but it's about creating a fulfilling and meaningful life through the resources that wealth provides.

Through the pages of this book, readers will learn about the principles and strategies of wealth creation, including budgeting, saving, investing, and building a network of successful business contacts. They will also discover the importance of adopting a positive mindset and cultivating habits and behaviors that lead to success.

But the purpose of this book goes beyond just providing practical advice. It's about empowering readers to take control of their financial lives and make choices that align with their values and aspirations. It's about helping them create a life of purpose and impact by using their wealth to pursue their passions and make a positive difference in the world.

Ultimately, the purpose of "Be Wealthy" is to inspire and guide readers to achieve their dreams of financial freedom and a wealthy lifestyle. By sharing the insights and experiences of successful individuals, this book shows that wealth is within reach for anyone who is willing to put in the effort and adopt the right mindset.

Introduction

Lena had always dreamed of having financial stability and freedom. Growing up, she had seen her parents struggle to make ends meet and live paycheck to paycheck. She didn't want to be in the same position, and so she made a commitment to herself to become financially independent.

Lena knew that wealth was not just about having a lot of money, but it was about having the resources to live a life that was fulfilling and meaningful. She wanted to be able to pursue her passions, travel the world, and give back to her community. She also knew that achieving financial success would require hard work and dedication.

She started by educating herself on financial management and wealth creation. She read books and articles, listened to podcasts, and attended seminars. She learned about budgeting, investing, and entrepreneurship. She also surrounded herself with successful and like-minded people who could guide and support her on her journey.

Lena took action and started implementing the strategies she had learned. She cut back on unnecessary expenses, created a budget, and started saving and investing her money. She also started a side business selling handmade crafts online, which helped to supplement her income.

However, the path to wealth was not always smooth sailing. Lena faced setbacks and obstacles, such as unexpected expenses and market downturns. But she remained committed to her goals and remained flexible in her approach. She adjusted her budget and investment portfolio, and she continued to work hard on her business.

Over time, Lena's wealth began to grow. She had built up a solid emergency fund, paid off her debt, and had investments that were generating passive income. She was able to travel to new places and pursue her passions, while also giving back to her community through volunteering and charitable donations.

Lena realized that achieving financial success was not just about having the right tools and strategies, but it was also about having the right mindset. She remained optimistic and determined, even during challenging times. She also stayed focused on her long-term goals and avoided getting sidetracked by short-term distractions.

In the end, Lena's journey to becoming wealthy taught her that with the right mindset, tools, and strategies, anyone can achieve financial success and live a fulfilling life. She continued to learn and grow throughout her life, and she never forgot the lessons she had learned on her journey to understanding wealth. She shared her knowledge and experience with others, inspiring them to pursue their own dreams of financial freedom and a wealthy lifestyle.

Table of Contents

Chapter 1: Understanding Wealth

Chapter 2: Creating a Wealth Mindset

Chapter 3: Building Wealth through Income

Chapter 4: Investing for Wealth

Chapter 5: Creating Multiple Streams of Income

Chapter 6: Building a Wealthy Lifestyle

Chapter 7: Overcoming Obstacles to Wealth

Chapter 8: Maintaining Wealth

Chapter 9 : Money Principles

Conclusion

Chapter 1:

Understanding Wealth

The first step in becoming wealthy is to understand what wealth is and what it means to be wealthy. Wealth is not just about having a lot of money, but it also encompasses other aspects such as good health, happiness, and fulfilling relationships. Being wealthy means having enough financial resources to meet your needs and desires, without worrying about money.

One real-life example of understanding wealth is the story of Robert Kiyosaki, author of the best-selling book "Rich Dad Poor Dad." Kiyosaki grew up with two father figures - his biological father, who was highly educated but struggled with money, and his best friend's father, who was a successful entrepreneur and investor. Through these two figures, Kiyosaki learned the importance of financial education and understanding how money works.

Kiyosaki started his own journey to wealth by investing in real estate and eventually creating his own educational materials to help others learn about personal finance and investing. He emphasizes the importance of having a financial plan and taking calculated risks to grow wealth over time.

Illustration

Once upon a time, in a small village nestled in the lush green hills, lived a young girl named Lily. She was a curious child who always had a lot of questions about the world around her. One day, Lily saw a wealthy merchant passing by her village in his luxurious carriage, pulled by two magnificent horses. The sight of the carriage filled her with wonder and amazement. She wondered what it would be like to have all that wealth and power.

Lily decided to ask her wise grandmother about wealth. Her grandmother smiled and asked her to sit beside her on the porch. "My dear child, wealth is not just about having a lot of money," she said. "It is about having enough resources to meet your needs and desires, without worrying about money."

Lily was confused. She thought that having a lot of money was the only way to be wealthy. Her grandmother sensed her confusion and explained, "Wealth is also about having good health, happiness, and fulfilling relationships. It is about living a life that is rich in experiences, knowledge, and wisdom."

Lily still had a lot of questions. Her grandmother smiled and said, "Let me tell you a story." She began,

"Once upon a time, there was a man named John who was very wealthy. He had a big house, fancy cars, and lots of money in the bank. However, John was not happy. He had no friends or family to share his wealth with, and he spent most of his time alone in his big mansion, feeling empty and unfulfilled.

On the other hand, there was a poor farmer named Tom who lived in a small hut with his family. He had very little money, but he was always happy and content. Tom had a loving wife, two children, and many friends in the village. He enjoyed spending time with them, sharing meals, and telling stories.

One day, John and Tom met at a village fair. They started talking, and John was surprised to see how happy and content Tom was despite having so little money. John realized that his pursuit of wealth had left him feeling empty and unfulfilled. He decided to change his ways and focus on the things that truly mattered in life.

From that day on, John started to invest his time and money in building meaningful relationships with his family, friends, and community. He volunteered at a local charity, joined a book club, and started to explore his passions and interests. He found that these experiences gave him a sense of purpose and fulfillment that money could never buy.

Lily listened to the story with rapt attention. She understood that wealth was not just about having a lot of money, but it was also about having good health, happiness, and fulfilling relationships. She decided to focus on these aspects of wealth and not just on accumulating money.

As Lily grew older, she remembered her grandmother's wise words and the story she had told her. She worked hard, saved money, invested wisely, and built meaningful relationships with her family and friends. She found that true wealth was not just about having a lot of money but was about living a life that was rich in experiences, knowledge, and wisdom."

The illustration for this chapter could be of Lily sitting on the porch with her wise grandmother, looking out at the lush green hills in the distance. There could be a small stream flowing nearby, and colorful flowers blooming around them. The story of John and Tom could be depicted in a small inset on the page, with John looking lonely and unfulfilled in his mansion, and Tom surrounded by his family and friends in his small hut. The illustration could convey the message that wealth is not just about having a lot of money, but it is also about having good health, happiness, and fulfilling relationships.

Here are some important principles to understand about wealth:

Wealth is not just about money: While having financial resources is an important aspect of wealth, it is not the only one. Other aspects, such as good health, fulfilling relationships, and a sense of purpose, are equally important.

Wealth is relative: What one person considers wealthy may not be the same for another person. It is important to define what wealth means to you and your personal financial goals.

Wealth is not a one-time event: Building wealth is a process that takes time, effort, and discipline. It is not just about reaching a certain financial milestone but also about maintaining it over time.

Wealth requires smart decision-making: Making informed decisions about your finances is critical to building and maintaining wealth. This includes managing your income, investing wisely, and avoiding unnecessary debt.

Wealth requires discipline and sacrifice: Building wealth often requires making sacrifices and avoiding instant gratification. It means living below your means, prioritizing your financial goals, and avoiding impulsive spending.

Wealth requires diversification: Investing in a range of assets, such as stocks, bonds, and real estate, helps to spread risk and increase the likelihood of long-term financial success.

Wealth requires continuous learning: Staying informed about financial trends, market conditions, and investment opportunities is essential to building and maintaining wealth. It requires a willingness to learn and adapt to changing circumstances.

Chapter 2:

Creating a Wealth Mindset

To become wealthy, you need to have a wealth mindset. This means believing in your ability to create wealth, developing a positive attitude towards money, and adopting habits and behaviors that align with your financial goals. Some of the key mindset shifts you need to make include overcoming limiting beliefs, embracing a growth mindset, and cultivating a sense of abundance.

Warren Buffett is widely regarded as one of the most successful investors of all time. He is a prime example of someone who embodies the principles of a wealth mindset. Buffett's journey towards becoming one of the wealthiest people in the world began at a young age.

As a child, Buffett was always interested in money and investing.

He started investing at the age of 11 when he purchased his first stock. By the time he was 13, he was running a small business delivering newspapers. He saved up his money and invested it in the stock market, which allowed him to continue to grow his wealth.

Buffett's positive attitude towards money and investing has been a key factor in his success. He believes in his ability to create wealth and has always maintained a sense of abundance, even during economic downturns. This positive mindset has allowed him to see opportunities where others might only see challenges.

One of the key mindset shifts that Buffett has emphasized is the importance of overcoming limiting beliefs. He has often spoken about the need to challenge your own assumptions and beliefs about money and investing. By doing so, you can open yourself up to new possibilities and opportunities.

Buffett has also emphasized the importance of embracing a growth mindset. He has continually learned and adapted to changing market conditions throughout his career. He has been willing to try new things and take calculated risks, which has allowed him to achieve great success.

Buffett's approach to investing is also a reflection of his wealth mindset. He is a long-term investor who focuses on buying undervalued companies with strong fundamentals. He is a disciplined investor who does not get caught up in short-term market fluctuations or hype. This approach has allowed him to generate consistently high returns over the long term.

Overall, Warren Buffett's success is a testament to the power of a wealth mindset. By believing in his ability to create wealth, maintaining a positive attitude towards money, and embracing a growth mindset, he has achieved extraordinary success in the world of investing. His story serves as an inspiration to anyone who is looking to build wealth and achieve financial independence.

Illustration

Once upon a time, there was a young man named Jack who lived in a small village in the countryside. Jack had always dreamed of becoming wealthy and living a life of luxury, but he didn't know where to start. He thought that the only way to become wealthy was to inherit money or win the lottery.

One day, Jack met a wise old man who was known for his wealth and success. The old man saw the determination in Jack's eyes and decided to share his secrets to success. He explained that to become wealthy, Jack needed to develop a wealth mindset. Jack was confused and asked the old man to explain what that meant.

The old man said, "To have a wealth mindset, you need to believe in your ability to create wealth. You need to have a positive attitude towards money and adopt habits and behaviors that align with your financial goals. You also need to overcome limiting beliefs, embrace a growth mindset, and cultivate a sense of abundance."

Jack listened carefully and asked the old man how he could make these mindset shifts. The old man smiled and said, "Let me show you."

The old man took Jack to a nearby farm and showed him a field of wheat. He asked Jack to count the number of wheat stalks in the field. Jack started counting and soon realized that there were too many to count. The old man smiled and said, "That's right. There are too many to count, but that doesn't mean there isn't enough to go around. Just like this field of wheat, the universe has an abundance of wealth. You just need to believe that it's there for you."

Jack was amazed by the old man's wisdom and started to shift his mindset. He started believing in his ability to create wealth and adopted positive habits and behaviors that aligned with his financial goals. He overcame his limiting beliefs and embraced a growth mindset.

Years went by, and Jack became a successful businessman. He created his own company and became one of the wealthiest men in the village. But he never forgot the old man's words and continued to cultivate a sense of abundance.

The illustration for this chapter could be of Jack standing in a field of wheat, looking up at the vast blue sky above. The wheat stalks could be depicted as symbols of wealth, with some tall and strong and others small and weak. The illustration could convey the message that just like the field of wheat, the universe has an abundance of wealth, and all we need to do is believe in our ability to create it.

Here are some principles to create a wealth mindset:

Believe in yourself: You must have faith in yourself and your ability to create wealth. A positive mindset is essential to building wealth.

Adopt a growth mindset: A growth mindset means embracing challenges and learning from failures. It's important to view setbacks as opportunities for growth rather than roadblocks.

Cultivate an abundance mindset: An abundance mindset means focusing on possibilities rather than limitations. It involves viewing the world as full of opportunities and having faith that there is always enough to go around.

Set clear financial goals: It's important to set clear and specific financial goals to provide direction and focus.

Practice gratitude: Practicing gratitude helps to shift your mindset towards abundance and away from scarcity. Being thankful for what you have can help you attract more positivity into your life.

Surround yourself with positive influences: Surrounding yourself with people who have a positive mindset towards money and success can help reinforce your own positive beliefs.

Take action towards your goals: Taking action towards your goals is essential to creating a wealth mindset. Small steps towards your financial goals can help build momentum and confidence.

Chapter 3:

Building Wealth through Income

One of the primary ways to build wealth is through your income. This chapter will explore various strategies for increasing your income, such as starting a side hustle, investing in yourself, negotiating for a higher salary, and creating passive income streams. We'll also discuss the importance of managing your income and budgeting effectively to maximize your wealth-building potential.

Oprah Winfrey is one of the most successful and wealthiest women in the world, and her success story is a testament to the power of building multiple streams of income. She started her career as a talk show host, and her show, "The Oprah Winfrey Show," quickly became one of the most successful talk shows in history. However, Winfrey did not stop there. She used her platform to build an empire that includes media, entertainment, and philanthropy.

One of the key ways that Winfrey has built wealth is by investing in herself. She has taken risks and pursued new opportunities, such as launching her own TV network, the Oprah Winfrey Network (OWN). When the network initially struggled to gain traction, Winfrey did not give up. Instead, she invested in the network and continued to promote it, eventually turning it into a successful venture.

Another way that Winfrey has built wealth is by negotiating for higher salaries. When she was first offered the role of Sofia in the movie "The Color Purple," Winfrey was told that she would be paid $35,000 for the role. However, she negotiated for a higher salary, eventually earning $250,000 for the role. This was a significant increase, and it set the stage for Winfrey to negotiate for higher salaries in the future.

In addition to investing in herself and negotiating for higher salaries, Winfrey has also built passive income streams through her investments. She has invested in various businesses, including Weight Watchers and a real estate venture with billionaire Jeff Greene. She has also invested in the stock market, including investments in companies like Apple and Amazon.

Winfrey's success is not just about building wealth, however. She has also used her platform and her wealth to make a difference in the world. She is a philanthropist, and she has donated millions of dollars to various causes, including education, healthcare, and disaster relief efforts.

Overall, Oprah Winfrey's success is a testament to the power of building multiple streams of income and investing in oneself. By taking risks, negotiating for higher salaries, and building passive income streams through investments, Winfrey has been able to build an empire that includes media, entertainment, and philanthropy.

Illustration

Once upon a time, there was a young woman named Maya who was determined to build wealth through her income. She worked a full-time job in marketing, but she knew that her salary alone wouldn't be enough to achieve her financial goals.

Maya decided to start a side hustle as a freelance writer, using her writing skills to generate additional income. She spent her evenings and weekends pitching articles to online publications and blogging about topics she was passionate about. Within a few months, Maya was able to secure several regular writing gigs, which brought in a significant amount of extra income.

But Maya didn't stop there. She also invested in herself by taking courses and attending workshops to improve her writing skills and learn new marketing techniques. As her expertise grew, so did her rates, allowing her to earn even more from her side hustle.

Maya also recognized the importance of negotiating for a higher salary at her full-time job. She researched industry standards and prepared a persuasive case for a raise, which she presented to her boss. To her delight, her boss agreed to the raise, boosting her income even further.

But Maya knew that relying solely on active income wasn't enough to achieve true wealth. So she began exploring ways to create passive income streams, such as investing in stocks and rental properties. She spent hours researching and analyzing potential investments, seeking out those with strong potential for long-term growth.

And with careful budgeting and management of her income, Maya was able to make the most of her financial resources. She automated her savings and investments, allowing her money to work for her even when she wasn't actively working. She also developed a frugal mindset, avoiding unnecessary expenses and focusing on living within her means.

Thanks to Maya's dedication and hard work, she was able to build wealth through her income, achieving financial stability and freedom. And she knew that her success was not just a matter of luck, but a result of her mindset, habits, and strategic planning.

Here are some principles of building wealth through income:

Increase your income: One of the simplest ways to build wealth through income is to increase your earning potential. This can be done through pursuing additional education or training, gaining new skills, or negotiating for a higher salary.

Start a side hustle: Starting a side business or freelance work can provide additional income and can also be a way to pursue your passions and interests.

Invest in yourself: Investing in your own personal and professional development can increase your earning potential and lead to opportunities for advancement.

Manage your income wisely: It's not just about how much you earn, but also how you manage your income. Creating a budget, minimizing expenses, and saving for the future can all help to build wealth over time.

Create passive income streams: Passive income streams, such as rental properties or investments in stocks, can provide ongoing income without requiring constant effort or attention.

Chapter 4:

Investing for Wealth

Investing is another key strategy for building wealth. In this chapter, we'll delve into the different investment options available, such as stocks, bonds, real estate, and alternative investments. We'll also discuss the importance of diversification, risk management, and having a long-term investment strategy.

Jack Bogle, who passed away in 2019, was a titan in the world of investing. He founded the Vanguard Group in 1974 and was instrumental in popularizing index investing, a strategy that has become increasingly popular in recent years.

At the heart of Bogle's approach to investing was the belief that low costs and diversification are the keys to success. He believed that most active managers were unable to consistently outperform the market, and that the fees they charged often ate into returns. Instead, he advocated for investing in a low-cost, passively managed index fund that tracks a market index, such as the S&P 500.

This approach to investing has proven to be highly effective over the long term. By investing in a diversified portfolio of stocks that track a market index, investors can achieve returns that are comparable to the overall market, while keeping costs low.

Bogle also emphasized the importance of having a long-term investment strategy. He believed that trying to time the market was a fool's errand, and that investors were better off staying the course and riding out market volatility. He often cited the example of the stock market crash of 1987, which saw the market drop by over 20% in a single day. While many investors panicked and sold their holdings, Bogle stayed the course and continued to invest in index funds. Over the long term, this approach paid off handsomely.

In addition to his investment philosophy, Bogle was also known for his advocacy on behalf of individual investors. He was a vocal critic of Wall Street and the financial industry, and often spoke out against excessive fees and conflicts of interest. He believed that the financial industry should be focused on serving the needs of investors, rather than enriching itself at their expense.

In recognition of his contributions to the world of investing, Bogle received numerous awards and accolades throughout his life. In 2017, he was inducted into the American Academy of Arts and Sciences, and in 2019 he was posthumously awarded the Presidential Medal of Freedom, the highest civilian honor in the United States.

Overall, Jack Bogle's approach to investing offers valuable lessons for anyone looking to build wealth through investing. By keeping costs low, diversifying investments, and adopting a long-term investment strategy, investors can achieve excellent returns over the long term, while minimizing the risk of losses due to market volatility.

Illustration

Meet Sarah, a young professional who has just received a significant bonus at work. She's excited about the prospect of using this money to build wealth, but she's not sure where to start. She decides to do some research on investing and comes across a book that outlines various investment options.

Sarah learns about the different types of investments, such as stocks, bonds, real estate, and alternative investments. She's intrigued by the potential returns of the stock market but is hesitant about the risks involved. She decides to start with a small investment in a diversified portfolio of stocks and bonds, using a robo-advisor to manage her portfolio.

As she continues to learn about investing, Sarah becomes more confident in her abilities and begins to explore other options. She learns about real estate investing and decides to invest in a rental property. She does her due diligence and researches the market, finding a property that she believes will generate a good return on investment.

Sarah also considers alternative investments, such as peer-to-peer lending and crowdfunding. She decides to invest in a renewable energy project through a crowdfunding platform, seeing the potential for both financial and environmental returns.

Through her investments, Sarah has built a diversified portfolio that balances risk and return. She's also developed a long-term investment strategy, with a focus on reinvesting her returns and continuing to grow her wealth over time.

As she reflects on her journey, Sarah realizes that investing is not just about making money but also about building a better future for herself and her loved ones. By taking the time to learn and explore different investment options, she has positioned herself for long-term financial success.

Here are some principles of Investing for Wealth:

Diversification: Don't put all your eggs in one basket. Diversify your portfolio by investing in different asset classes, such as stocks, bonds, and real estate.

Risk Management: Assess the risk associated with each investment and make informed decisions. Don't put all your money into high-risk investments without understanding the potential consequences.

Long-term Perspective: Investing is a long-term game. Don't get caught up in short-term fluctuations in the market. Focus on your long-term investment goals and stick to your strategy.

Research and Analysis: Do your due diligence before investing in any asset. Research the company or property, analyze the market trends, and consult with experts if necessary.

Patience: Investing requires patience. Don't expect quick returns on your investments. Stay committed to your strategy and give your investments time to grow.

Regular Review: Regularly review your investment portfolio and make adjustments if necessary. Stay informed about market trends and be prepared to adapt to changes.

Discipline: Stick to your investment plan and resist the temptation to make impulsive decisions. Develop a disciplined approach to investing and stick to it.

Chapter 5:

Creating Multiple Streams of Income

To truly become wealthy, you need to have multiple streams of income. This chapter will explore various ways to create additional income streams, such as starting a business, investing in rental properties, and building a passive income portfolio. We'll also discuss the importance of having a plan for each income stream and monitoring your progress towards your wealth goals.

When we think of Elon Musk, the first thing that comes to mind is his innovative and disruptive ideas. He is the man behind Tesla, SpaceX, Neuralink, and The Boring Company. But Musk's achievements don't stop there. He has also mastered the art of creating multiple streams of income, which has allowed him to build wealth while pursuing his passions.

Musk started his career as an entrepreneur, co-founding PayPal, an online payment system, which was later acquired by eBay. This was just the beginning of his journey towards financial success. He went on to found several other successful companies, including Tesla, which revolutionized the automotive industry with its electric cars, and SpaceX, which is working towards making space travel more accessible.

Musk's success as an entrepreneur is not limited to these companies alone. He has also invested in rental properties, and has a stake in several other businesses, including SolarCity, which provides solar energy solutions, and OpenAI, an artificial intelligence research institute. By diversifying his income streams, Musk has been able to build a fortune, estimated at over $200 billion, and secure his place among the world's wealthiest individuals.

One of Musk's most significant achievements is his ability to align his passions with his investments. He is not only focused on building wealth but also on creating a better future for humanity. His work with Tesla and SpaceX aims to reduce our dependence on fossil fuels and make space travel more accessible, respectively. By investing in companies that share his vision, Musk has been able to combine his passions with his financial goals.

Another factor that sets Musk apart is his willingness to take risks. He has invested heavily in companies that many others would have considered too risky, such as SpaceX, which required significant investments in rocket technology. However, his investments have paid off, as these companies have become successful and profitable.

Musk's success also highlights the importance of creating passive income streams. While his companies require a lot of work and attention, his investments in rental properties and other businesses provide a source of income that requires little effort once established. This allows Musk to focus on his passions and continue to pursue innovative ideas.

In conclusion, Elon Musk is a prime example of someone who has mastered the art of creating multiple streams of income. He has diversified his investments, aligned his passions with his financial goals, taken risks, and created passive income streams. Musk's success is a testament to the power of a diversified income portfolio and the benefits of investing in companies that align with your values and passions.

Illustration

Meet Alex, a young entrepreneur who has always dreamed of becoming wealthy. Alex has a full-time job, but realizes that relying on just one income stream won't be enough to achieve his financial goals. He decides to explore different ways of creating multiple streams of income.

Alex starts by researching different business ideas and finds one that aligns with his passion for healthy living. He creates a website and starts a blog about healthy eating and lifestyle habits. He monetizes the blog through affiliate marketing and sponsorships. This becomes his first additional income stream.

Next, Alex decides to invest in rental properties. He saves up enough money for a down payment on a small apartment complex and hires a property management company to handle the day-to-day tasks. He rents out the apartments at a profitable rate and starts generating a steady stream of passive income.

Finally, Alex starts building a passive income portfolio by investing in dividend-paying stocks and mutual funds. He uses his knowledge of the market to make smart investment decisions and diversifies his portfolio to minimize risk.

Over time, Alex's income streams start to grow and compound. He continues to monitor his progress and adjusts his plans as necessary. With each additional stream of income, Alex moves closer to his goal of financial independence and wealth.

Through his journey, Alex learns the importance of having a plan for each income stream and monitoring his progress towards his wealth goals. He also realizes that creating multiple streams of income takes hard work, dedication, and persistence, but the rewards are worth it in the end.

Some principles of creating multiple streams of income include:

Diversification: Creating multiple streams of income helps to diversify your sources of revenue and reduces your dependence on a single income stream.

Focus on your strengths: Identify your unique skills, strengths, and passions to create income streams that align with your interests and expertise.

Find opportunities: Look for opportunities to monetize your skills and knowledge through various means such as freelancing, consulting, or starting a side hustle.

Develop a plan: Create a plan for each income stream that includes specific goals, timelines, and metrics to measure progress and success.

Monitor progress: Regularly track your income streams and adjust your strategies based on what's working and what's not.

Be patient: Creating multiple streams of income takes time and effort. It requires persistence and patience to build up each stream and see the results over the long term.

Leverage technology: Embrace technology and use it to your advantage in creating and managing your income streams. This could include using online platforms to market your services or automate certain tasks.

Chapter 6:

Building a Wealthy Lifestyle

Building a wealthy lifestyle means living below your means, focusing on your values, and making intentional decisions about how you spend your money. This chapter will explore the habits and behaviors of wealthy individuals, such as saving, investing, and prioritizing experiences over material possessions. We'll also discuss the importance of giving back and being socially responsible as part of a wealthy lifestyle.

Bill Gates is a household name, not just for his incredible business acumen, but also for his philanthropic work and his modest lifestyle. Despite being one of the richest people in the world, he has always maintained a simple and frugal lifestyle, which is a testament to his values.

Gates' frugality and focus on his values have been evident since the early days of Microsoft. In the early years of the company, he famously used to sleep under his desk to save on rent, and he continued to maintain a simple lifestyle even as his wealth grew.

One of the key ways that Gates has built a wealthy lifestyle is by living below his means. Despite being worth billions of dollars, he still flies coach and drives a modest car. This is a stark contrast to many other billionaires who spend exorbitant amounts of money on luxury goods and experiences.

In fact, Gates once said in an interview, "I have all the toys I could ever want, and I just don't see the point in spending money on things that won't make a difference in the world."

Gates' focus on his values is also evident in his philanthropic work. Along with his wife, Melinda Gates, he has pledged to give away a significant portion of his wealth to various causes, including global health, education, and climate change. Their foundation, the Bill and Melinda Gates Foundation, is one of the largest charitable organizations in the world.

Gates has also prioritized experiences over material possessions, choosing to spend time with his family and friends rather than accumulating more wealth. He has talked about how he enjoys playing bridge with his friends, going on walks with his wife, and spending time with his children.

In summary, Bill Gates is an excellent example of someone who has built a wealthy lifestyle by living below his means, focusing on his values, and prioritizing experiences over material possessions. His frugality and commitment to philanthropy are an inspiration to many, and his success is a testament to the fact that true wealth is not just about accumulating money but about living a fulfilling and purposeful life.

Illustration

Sarah had always been intrigued by the idea of building a wealthy lifestyle for herself. She had read books and articles on the subject, and even attended a few seminars, but still felt overwhelmed by the idea of where to start.

That's when she stumbled upon Chapter 6 of a book she had been reading. It was all about building a wealthy lifestyle through intentional living, and it really resonated with her.

She began by taking a closer look at her spending habits and identifying areas where she could cut back. Sarah realized that she had been spending a lot of money on material possessions that didn't really bring her much joy, and decided to start prioritizing experiences instead.

She also started saving a portion of her income each month and investing it in a diversified portfolio. It was a small step, but she knew that over time it would add up and help her build long-term wealth.

As Sarah continued to live intentionally, she started to notice a shift in her mindset. She no longer felt the need to keep up with the latest trends or impress others with her possessions. Instead, she focused on her values and what truly made her happy.

In addition to her personal wealth-building efforts, Sarah also started giving back to her community through volunteering and donating to charities. She realized that being wealthy didn't just mean accumulating more money, but also using it to make a positive impact on the world.

Through her intentional living and focus on building a wealthy lifestyle, Sarah found a newfound sense of purpose and fulfillment. She was able to live a life that aligned with her values and priorities, while also creating a solid foundation for long-term wealth.

Here are some principles of building a wealthy lifestyle:

Live below your means: Spend less than you earn and avoid debt.

Prioritize your values: Focus on what truly matters to you and spend your money accordingly.

Invest in yourself: Continuously improve your skills and knowledge to increase your earning potential.

Save and invest: Create a budget and save a portion of your income for the future. Invest wisely to grow your wealth.

Prioritize experiences over possessions: Spend money on experiences that create memories and joy rather than material possessions.

Give back: Make a positive impact in your community and the world by supporting causes that align with your values.

Be socially responsible: Consider the impact of your actions on others and the environment, and make choices that benefit society as a whole.

Focus on long-term goals: Have a plan for your future and make decisions that support your long-term financial goals.

Chapter 7:

Overcoming Obstacles to Wealth

Becoming wealthy is not always easy, and there are many obstacles along the way. In this chapter, we'll explore common obstacles to wealth, such as debt, procrastination, and fear of failure. We'll also discuss strategies for overcoming these obstacles and staying on track towards your financial goals.

J.K. Rowling is a name synonymous with success and inspiration. Her journey from a struggling single mother to one of the most successful authors in the world is a testament to her resilience, perseverance, and determination. Rowling's story is an excellent example of how overcoming obstacles is crucial to achieving wealth and success.

Before her success, Rowling went through a period of immense hardship. After separating from her husband, she found herself in a state of poverty, struggling to make ends meet. She was living on government benefits and had to rely on food banks to feed herself and her daughter. However, despite her struggles, she never gave up on her dream of becoming a writer.

Rowling began writing the first Harry Potter book while she was still living in poverty, and it was not an easy journey. She faced rejection after rejection from publishers, and it was only after the eighth publisher that she finally got her big break. Even after her book was published, Rowling continued to face challenges. She had to balance being a single mother and a successful writer, often writing late into the night after her daughter had gone to bed.

However, despite these obstacles, Rowling persisted, and her hard work eventually paid off. The Harry Potter series became a global phenomenon, selling millions of copies worldwide and inspiring a generation of readers. Rowling's success allowed her to achieve financial stability and security for herself and her family.

In addition to her success, Rowling has also been open about her struggles with mental health. She has spoken publicly about her battles with depression and the importance of seeking help when needed. By doing so, she has helped to break the stigma surrounding mental health and has inspired others to seek help and support when facing similar struggles.

In conclusion, J.K. Rowling's story is a powerful example of how overcoming obstacles is crucial to achieving wealth and success. Her perseverance, determination, and willingness to seek help when needed are all traits that have contributed to her success. Rowling's journey is a reminder that, no matter what obstacles we face, with hard work and determination, we can achieve our goals and create a better future for ourselves and those around us.

Illustration

Once upon a time, there was a young woman named Lily who dreamed of becoming wealthy. She worked hard and saved diligently, but she kept encountering obstacles that held her back.

One day, Lily found herself in a deep hole of debt. She had taken out loans to fund her education and had accumulated credit card debt from overspending. She felt overwhelmed and discouraged, but she knew she couldn't give up on her goal of wealth.

Lily turned to her mentor, an experienced investor named John, for advice. He reminded her that debt was a common obstacle to wealth and that there were strategies she could use to overcome it. John suggested that Lily prioritize paying off her debts with the highest interest rates first and then gradually work her way down.

Lily took John's advice and started making extra payments on her high-interest debts while cutting back on her expenses. She also picked up a side hustle as a freelance writer to earn additional income. It wasn't easy, but over time, Lily was able to pay off her debts and become debt-free.

However, Lily soon faced another obstacle: procrastination. She had a tendency to put off important tasks, like investing in stocks or starting her own business, because she was afraid of failure. She feared that if she made a mistake, she would lose all her hard-earned money.

John reminded Lily that failure was a natural part of the wealth-building process and that successful investors often made mistakes along the way. He suggested that Lily start small by investing in low-risk stocks and gradually work her way up. John also encouraged Lily to focus on her long-term goals and not to get discouraged by short-term setbacks.

With John's guidance, Lily started investing in stocks and eventually started her own side business selling handmade crafts. Though she encountered some bumps along the way, she remained persistent and focused on her long-term goals. Over time, her investments grew, and her business became profitable, bringing in additional income.

In the end, Lily overcame her obstacles to wealth by tackling her debt, overcoming her fear of failure, and staying focused on her goals. She had built a strong foundation for her financial future and could look forward to a life of wealth and abundance.

Here are some principles for overcoming obstacles to wealth:

Take responsibility: Acknowledge that you are responsible for your financial situation and take ownership of it.

Develop a growth mindset: Embrace a growth mindset and believe that you can improve your financial situation through learning, hard work, and persistence.

Create a plan: Develop a plan for achieving your financial goals and break it down into actionable steps.

Focus on solutions, not problems: Instead of dwelling on the obstacles, focus on finding solutions and taking action towards your goals.

Surround yourself with positivity: Surround yourself with people who support your goals and have a positive attitude towards wealth.

Continuously educate yourself: Stay informed and continuously educate yourself about financial topics and investment strategies.

Learn from mistakes: View setbacks and failures as learning opportunities and adjust your approach accordingly.

Be patient: Building wealth takes time and patience. Stay committed to your plan and don't give up.

Chapter 8:

Maintaining Wealth

Finally, building wealth is not just about reaching a financial milestone but also about maintaining it over time. This chapter will explore the habits and behaviors of wealthy individuals that help them maintain their wealth, such as diversification, risk management, and continuous learning. We'll also discuss the importance of having a plan for your wealth and preparing for unexpected events.

Jeff Bezos is another example of someone who has built and maintained wealth over time. Bezos started Amazon as an online bookstore in 1994 and has since grown it into one of the largest e-commerce companies in the world, with a market capitalization of over $1 trillion. Bezos has also diversified his income streams by investing in other businesses, such as Blue Origin, a space exploration company, and The Washington Post, a newspaper.

Bezos has been known for his long-term vision and willingness to take risks, which has allowed him to create a company that has disrupted traditional retail and transformed the way people shop online. He has also focused on customer satisfaction, investing heavily in logistics and delivery to provide fast and reliable service.

Bezos has also demonstrated the importance of staying focused on the long-term and not getting distracted by short-term fluctuations in the market. He has maintained a strong commitment to his vision for Amazon and has continued to invest in new products and services, even when they may not have an immediate impact on the company's bottom line. This has allowed Amazon to maintain its position as a leader in e-commerce and expand into new markets and industries.

Illustration

Once upon a time, there was a successful business owner named Sarah. She had worked hard to build her business, and over time, she had accumulated a significant amount of wealth. However, she was not content with just reaching this milestone; she wanted to maintain her wealth and continue growing it for years to come.

Sarah knew that maintaining wealth was not easy, and there

were many challenges along the way. She had seen many people who had lost their wealth due to poor financial decisions or unexpected events. To avoid such pitfalls, Sarah was determined to develop the habits and behaviors of wealthy individuals.

First, she understood the importance of diversification. She had learned from her own experience that it was not wise to put all her eggs in one basket. Instead, she invested in a broad range of assets, such as stocks, bonds, real estate, and alternative investments. This way, even if one asset class performed poorly, she had other investments that could offset the losses.

Second, Sarah was committed to risk management. She knew that investing always involved some level of risk, but she also knew that she could mitigate that risk by making smart investment decisions. She regularly monitored her investments, paid attention to market trends, and sought the advice of financial experts when needed.

Third, Sarah was always learning. She knew that the world of finance was constantly changing, and she needed to stay ahead of the curve to maintain her wealth. She read books and articles on investing, attended seminars and conferences, and sought out the advice of successful investors.

Finally, Sarah had a plan for her wealth. She knew that unexpected events could happen at any time, and she wanted to be prepared. She had set up a trust for her family, had adequate insurance coverage, and had made sure that her business had a solid succession plan in place.

As a result of these habits and behaviors, Sarah was able to maintain her wealth over time. She was confident in her financial decisions and knew that she was well-prepared for any unexpected events that might arise. She was grateful for the opportunities that her wealth had provided her and was committed to using it for good, whether by supporting charitable causes or investing in new business ventures.

In conclusion, building and maintaining wealth requires a long-term perspective and a commitment to developing the habits and behaviors of successful investors. By diversifying investments, managing risk, continuously learning, and having a plan in place, individuals can maintain their wealth and continue to grow it for years to come.

Here are some principles for maintaining wealth:

Diversification: Spread your investments across different asset classes to reduce risk and increase potential returns.

Risk Management: Manage risk by understanding your investments, setting realistic expectations, and creating a plan for potential losses.

Continuous Learning: Stay informed about changes in the market, new investment opportunities, and financial strategies to improve your wealth-building potential.

Long-Term Focus: Keep a long-term perspective when it comes to your investments and wealth-building strategies. Avoid short-term thinking that can lead to impulsive decisions.

Planning: Create a financial plan that takes into account your goals, income, expenses, and risk tolerance. Review and adjust your plan regularly to ensure it remains relevant.

Preparation: Plan for unexpected events such as job loss, illness, or market downturns by having an emergency fund and insurance in place.

Patience: Building and maintaining wealth is a long-term process that requires patience, discipline, and consistent effort.

Money Principles

Sure, here are five formulas with money principles used by rich people to build wealth through income:

Start a Side Hustle: One of the best ways to increase your income is by starting a side hustle. Many wealthy people have multiple streams of income, and a side hustle can help you achieve this. Look for ways to monetize your skills, talents, or hobbies. For example, you could start a freelance business, sell products online, or offer consulting services.

Money Principle: Diversify your income streams to increase your overall earning potential.

Invest in Yourself: Investing in yourself is one of the best investments you can make. Take courses, attend seminars, and read books to improve your skills and knowledge. The more you invest in yourself, the more valuable you become to employers, clients, and customers. This can lead to higher paying job opportunities or the ability to charge more for your services.

Money Principle: Invest in your education and skills to increase your earning potential.

Negotiate for a Higher Salary: If you're currently employed, negotiating for a higher salary is a great way to increase your income. Do your research on industry standards and the value you bring to the company. Make a case for why you deserve a raise, and be willing to negotiate. Remember, if you don't ask, you don't receive.

Money Principle: Don't be afraid to negotiate for a higher salary to maximize your earning potential.

Create Passive Income Streams: Passive income is money earned without actively working for it. This can include rental income from real estate, royalties from creative works, or dividend income from investments. Creating passive income streams can be a great way to build wealth over time.

Money Principle: Create passive income streams to earn money even when you're not actively working.

Manage Your Income and Budget Effectively: Managing your income and budgeting effectively is crucial for building wealth. Make a budget and stick to it, track your expenses, and look for ways to save money. This will help you avoid overspending and allow you to invest in your future.

Money Principle: Manage your income and budget effectively to maximize your wealth-building potential.

Conclusion:

Becoming wealthy is a journey that requires effort, discipline, and dedication. However, with the right mindset, tools, and strategies, anyone can achieve financial success and live a wealthy lifestyle. By adopting the habits and behaviors of wealthy individuals, you can build a prosperous future for yourself and your loved ones.

www.ingramcontent.com/pod-product-compliance
Lightning Source LLC
Chambersburg PA
CBHW040359220526
45473CB00025B/2591